Praise for
The Jeshua Collective

I am overwhelmed with tears of joy at the information that was given to me about my mother. I have found someone that I can trust with readings.

Jeshua Collective validated my mediumship abilities and walked me through what was happening with my own awakening. I was afraid of what was happening, I no longer feel paranoid. I am looking forward to the future instead of dread. It is heartwarming to know I have abilities. Thank you Jeshua.

Jeshua is undeniably speaking through Carol. She (they) knew things about my life that is not on social media or available publicly. I am able to heal myself from my past and their guidance is undoubtedly the reason why.

I was hesitant to get a reading over the phone about my loved one but within the first 30 seconds there was information that came through that was incredibly accurate. Personality traits, physical issues, and words spoken before he passed. I am eternally grateful for finding Carol and her guides.

I wanted to truly thank you for such an amazing I AM weekend. I am beyond grateful for having the opportunity to receive healing from Jeshua and to also embrace new life experiences that were much needed for me. My heart is overflowing with tears of joy as I move in my life. I cannot thank you enough!!

All I can say is I hope I never miss an opportunity to attend the I AM Intensive weekends. I feel different, less stressed. Things just don't bother me anymore. I'm working on bringing my husband to one of them!

I can't thank you enough for what you do. The world needs to know the ACIM study group Spiritually Led Journey exists. Of all the ACIM groups I've belonged to, none have brought channeled conversation from Jesus to it to answer my questions. I feel blessed to have found you, Carol. Thank you for what you do.

Carol, I feel so blessed to have found you. The channeled reading I had with you changed my life. You are the real deal.

Thank you Carol for a great healing of my Dad's condition. He felt better immediately. I'm happy for the serendipity of life's unfoldment.

Ocularity OF THE MIND

The Gateway to Your Spiritual Development and Advancement of Your Intuitive Abilities

———— Ocularity Series ————
Book 1

CAROL COLLINS

Original Channel for The Jeshua Collective

Powerful You!
PUBLISHING
Sharing Wisdom ~ Shining Light

Ocularity of the Mind
The Gateway to Your Spiritual Development and
Advancement of Your Intuitive Abilities

The intent of the author is to provide general information to individuals who are taking positive steps in their lives for emotional and spiritual well-being. If you use any of the information in this book for yourself, the author and the publisher assume no responsibility for your actions. Readers are encouraged to seek the counsel of competent professionals with regards to such matters.

Powerful You! Publishing is committed to publishing works of quality and integrity. In that spirit, we are proud to offer this book to our readers; however, the story, the experiences, and the words are the author's alone.

Published by: Powerful You! Inc. USA
powerfulyoupublishing.com

Library of Congress Control Number: 2022919567

Carol Collins– First Edition

ISBN: 978-1-959348-01-6

First Edition October 2022

BODY MIND & SPIRIT / Channeling & Mediumship

Books Written by Jeshua

Book 1 - *Ocularity of the Mind (2022)*

At this publishing of this book there are 14 additional completed channeled works that are in queue for publishing with more on the way. To stay in contact with us, please subscribe via the website:

www.thepittsburghmedium.com

Dedication

To the Beings within the Jeshua Collective
who guided me into my own Unfoldment,
without whom I would not be who I am today.

To my parents, Daniel and Sharon Doerr, with whom I
now have a nonphysical-physical relationship with that
I am beyond thankful for. There are no words to express
how much they are helping to guide me as a channel and
in life from where they are now.

Last but not least, to my daughters Elizabeth, Amanda,
and Emma—in the order in which they graced my life.
You are loved, you are loving, and I love who you
are becoming. I didn't know it when you were growing
up, but I know it now—each of you have Soul Intentions
that are meaningful to your Higher Self. With this understanding, it is now my parenting goal to be there for you
in a new way, a way that compliments you as an adult,
and a way that includes receiving Guidance first.
I love you beyond measure.

Table of Contents

The Essential Material
The Four Pillars of Learning

PILLAR 1: The Foundational Material - the starting point for understanding who «Source Beings» are, who we are, and why we are having this life experience.

PILLAR 2: Idea Reconstruction - otherwise known as law of attraction, deliberate creation, verbal therapy, and using the power of thought energy to manifest your life, on purpose.

PILLAR 3: Directed Energy for Self-Healing - moving Source Frequency within "the grid" as a means of clearing unconscious beliefs that stop and/or delay your ability to connect with your Guide team and manifest a life of abundance.

PILLAR 4: Intuitive Development - verbal and vibrational instruction to open your inter-mind to ocular (mind's eye) to increase your ability to receive, clarity in that receiving, and accuracy on what your Guide is conveying to you.

A Pillar 4 Book

---

*Written in 6 video sessions
in a total of 18 hours.*

The Introduction

Channeled August 9, 2022

Ocularity of the Mind is a book not written by a human being, but without the human being it could not be written. Spoken out loud, word by word, the information was documented accurately. We did remove some personal guidance sprinkled here and there. The editing was completed after the book was. We have agreed with every edit. Let it be known that certain things are capitalized at our request and they are consistent throughout the book.

We are Teachers and Healers and we do have a body of knowledge that we plan to teach through—we like to call her "this girl"—and there is a funny story behind that. Her name is Carol Collins. She has surpassed what she built into this life to do as a channel. She built in to write books with us, but her personality says, "Yeah, but I also want… he or she did it that way and I want that too." It is a personality trait that is helpful for you all. And so we have added in-person events and we like those as well.

Surpassing your Intentions is okay with us! Your birth Intentions, your Soul Plan, is not a limitation; it is a starting point and you have starting points in many different categories. Communicating with us is just one category. When you are off your life Plan an internal clock starts buzzing and you feel drawn to change your life. Wouldn't it be nice, though, to hear a voice guiding you instead? We think so. It is the ultimate goal for each and every one of you—built into your Soul Plan or not. One by one, two by two, ten by ten, a thousand by a thousand, your humanness will alter itself back to knowing how to communicate verbally with your Guide.

Basic lessons are good for anyone. But what is the fastest, best way to get there? We show you how.

The Essential Material is woven in such a way to expand your minds, to improve your ability to translate for us clean, clear, and most especially accurate. Let it be known first and foremost, you are loved, you are tended to, and you are guided—every second of every day for your entire lives.

You laugh when people laugh, you cry when people cry, you grieve but you should not because it harms you. Secondly, your Loved Ones are perfect now. That is a question we get often so we like to put it in writing. Yes, they are okay and you will be too. Your physical life will be as well when you absorb the knowledge within these pages.

We love you so much. Take notes, write in the margins, dog-ear the pages, and be aware of your bodies! You just might (wink here, please—meaning you will) feel physical sensations caused by us (after chapter five for all of you and, for a good many, after chapter one). We have our eye on you while you are reading it. Ask for our help in absorbing the information and it will soak in faster. We like tips, tools, and techniques—this is one of them.

Come see us when you can at a live event. Shake hands with Carol and say hello to us because she likes that very much.

Ocularity of the Mind is a primer, it is the basics and there is always more to come. That is all.

Love,
Jeshua et al

CHAPTER 1

Opening to Channel

*"We want you to not worry about your thoughts
nor your emotions in any situation but just
keep going, keep going, keep going,
keep going, keep going, keep going,
keep going, keep going, keep going.
Because when you do, you will eventually come
upon one idea or choice that just feels good—
and then stay there."*

Session 1
Channeled April 11, 2021

There are so many thoughts that go on in the mind. This woman, Carol, she is sitting outside on her balcony and the sun is coming toward her. It is hard for her to keep her eyes open; she is squinting. She cannot see what is on the computer screen as she videotapes this dictation. She wanted to work out here; we know that she will get more done if she works inside, but she likes the fresh air.

There is something internally going on, yesterday and today, with her where she just needs to be outside. She took a long walk this morning, longer than she planned to, but it was a delightful walk. Then she came home and moved about the house, then did yoga. She began to do a yoga class on Gaia, and it felt, well, she got to the point where the woman was doing a lot of crunches and then it just felt like calisthenics and not yoga. So she said to us that she preferred to do yoga with us. We said, "Absolutely!" and then we began to move her body into the sun salutations that she loves so much.

She is a human being, and it is endearing to watch her move about. She then did one more thing, she went upstairs to go—"putz around," really. She began doing some odds and ends around the house and then her father, who passed away last year, said "blue jeans" to her, which she heard clearly in her mind. Without thinking or considering how strange it must be should someone hear her answering nobody, Carol said out loud, "Oh no, no, I think I'm going to wear yoga pants today" and he replied, "Okay." She wondered though why he said blue jeans. She knows she hears us accurately and was curious why her father's knowing was so much different than her own.

She looked down at the bench that is near the bed and she saw, sticking out of a bag, this lovely little blouse that she has on now. With excitement, she said, "Ohhh! I could wear that today," and so she put it on. She also got out her black leggings because she was thinking she was going to just stay in yoga pants all day and relax while doing video work. And then we said, "Blue jeans." At that moment she understood fully what her father was telling her. It was the picture he placed in her mind that made the "verbalness" clear. The image she saw was a picture of herself fully dressed in jeans and the yellow blouse and it looked good to her in her mind. She then had this instant second vision of walking one block over to the new restaurant that is right in her neighborhood and having lunch outside, or perhaps dinner. She reached into the cabinet where her jeans are and, looking through the pile said, "Oh, not those, not those," as you all do, and then, "Oh, I could go wear those! The ones that are all ripped up, those will look perfect!"

So she is here in this pretty little blouse and she has (remarkably) blue jeans on. She looks down and sees her beautiful sandals, the high-heel kind. Brown. Casual. The Saturday effect on her Sunday and she said, "Yep, that's what I'm going do today—videos, and then dinner outside."

So she got dressed and she came downstairs and then decided to add transcribing to her to-do list. We have a lot of books going through her. Know this to be true: we write through her as often as she will sit down for it. On the longer-than-usual walk she did this morning, we gave her two more titles. She has a list going.

She has many things that she wants to do, all of you do, but then she comes out here on the balcony in the fresh air. She is determined to sit on her balcony because she loved the one she had in her high-rise apartment in Alexandria. She loved living there. The balcony was quaint—perfect, really—although it was a tight squeeze, apartment-sized. But she loved it. She sat out there frequently in the afternoons and when the weather became too hot she simply shifted her balcony time to the early morning. She rarely missed a meal in the evening there.

So here she is on this day, Sunday, April 11, 2021 at 10:45 a.m. The sun keeps going behind the clouds and then comes out, and behind the clouds and then comes out. She sits down at the computer and says, "I cannot see a darn thing. You (meaning us) can close my eyes (during dictation), I know you do it sometimes, but I don't know if I want to do that the whole time (during videotaping)." And so she moves furniture around instead so that she is not looking into the sun and then she realizes that the video is too dark. So she moved back to where she was to begin with, sat down, and said, "Well, I could put sunglasses on."

Oh, people, you are so funny. You do not know where your words come from. You do not know where your thoughts come from. Every thought that you have ever thought remains. Sometimes you can push them down far enough that you do not know the thought exists, but they are always there and they are the cause for what you do, what you say, what you think, how you behave. Even the most minor of situations are all formed and shaped by the experiences you have taken in. This cause-and-effect is not a bad thing, it simply happens to be life as you know it. "Happens to be" is an interesting statement, is it not? We say it is the cause. It is not life. It is not real.

When Carol finally settles on furniture configuration, she says, "Well, maybe I'll start with my sunglasses off and put them back on when I begin to squint. I want the video to be clear." She has this visualization of herself far in the future, where people are re-watching her archive of videos. She is creating her reality then (future her) and now. Then, because it might turn out that way. Now, because the image is so strong in her that she has to adjust to accommodate a viewer that has not currently manifested. She knows this but the tendency to forecast this video being seen is something that she cannot overlook. Human tendency is what we are talking about here.

Then she goes over to the drawer in the kitchen and she sees the glasses that belonged to her father and she decided against them because they did not match. This is a quieted mind we are talking about. Her thoughts are consistently active. *I want this, not that, maybe this, or this, but not that.* That is a lot of what we will continually call "thinking thoughts."

These thoughts that you think—we love you so much. There are many of us in the Jeshua Collective. It is a book that we have all contributed to. With much consternation, she is allowing us to use the name Jeshua as the title for the Collective of beings that teach through her. We teach humanistic behavior and why thoughts matter a great deal.

It is the *only* thing that matters because thoughts create your reality.

We continue. Carol opened the drawer to where she has her little nest of sunglasses. Although different in each home, she always has, everywhere she goes, one area that is a little cluttered—a nest. But it is neatly cluttered. For her, it is always a nest of sunglasses. There is a little nook as well in the car that has sunglasses in it. She likes to say that her car is always perfectly clean except for that messy nook. As she says, "It reminds me that I am a regular human being."

So here again—keeping the theme going of Carol and her idiosyncrasies—she is in the apartment in Alexandria, and she has this delightful little wine fridge that she keeps her Perrier in and on top of it is the nest of sunglasses. Never messy, but a collection to choose from. They are bundled, more like a random collection. She cannot handle clutter for long and avoids it. Here in this new home in Pittsburgh, she has not found where to place her nest of sunglasses yet, so she puts them in a drawer. It is a very organized nest, albeit hidden, nonetheless.

She knows exactly where she keeps the sunglass nest but does not remember which ones are there and which are in the car. She assumed her favorite black ones were there yet as she opened the drawer she found a brown pair, favorite ones if you were to ask the inner mind. Interestingly enough, she had forgotten about them. Walking back to the front porch she remarked how perfect the brown sunglasses paired with her outfit. Had she chosen black shoes or jewelry she would not have felt strongly that this brown pair was perfectly paired with her clothes.

This is an example of how intricately delicate the human mind is. Not fragile, but delicate. It absorbs easily that which you experience. Once experienced, it shapes you, forms inside your mind as assumption, interior rhetoric that you must adhere to because it becomes who you are. Although you do not know this, even these words are shaping who you are. As you read this book, do recognize that we are storytelling a bit—well, a lot, to be sure—but we do so deliberately. We tell a story and then challenge your mind to listen to the rest of the story—to reframe it in the midst of shaping. It is what we do through this woman. We teach, we re-organize the thoughts and the emotions that go along with the thoughts to assist you in a way that you have not yet experienced. We alter your experience by talking you through an idea.

We want you to float through an experience, using this woman's experience. Carol made a decision (a soft decision, as it was but that is not always the case) on yoga pants, swiftly shifted based on an image received in the mind, then capitalized on that rather than sinking into indecision. This is good for you to re-read. You can move through emotion and choose which one to settle on. Curiosity, fun, thoughtfulness, happy.

We want you to not worry about your thoughts nor your emotions in any situation but just keep going, keep going, keep going, keep going, keep going, keep going, keep going, keep going, keep going. Because when you do, you will eventually come upon one idea or choice that just feels good—and then stay there. Let the good emotion wash over you. Let it refresh you. Let it be that dot-point of your day where you shifted completely from neutral or negative to happy. And then step off from there. The reason Carol was able to shift so easily on this day is because we have a daily practice of meditation, teaching moments, and attunements that clear the mind's retention of emotional thoughts. This is what allowed her to pay attention to the voice and the images in her mind's eye.

These thoughts that you have in your mind, they are interior thoughts that rise up. You just have them; you do not know where they come from. Sometimes you evaluate them, analyze yourself. Do not do it, but if you do, do it quickly and then simply say, "Hmm, isn't that interesting? I am a person. I love being a person. I think being a person is pretty fun. My Being (capitalized by Jeshua) must really love being a person because I am here, and I would not be here if I did not think that becoming a person would be fun." Because that is how it works—all of you have chosen to be here in this body in this life in this world. This activity or ones like it will help you discard emotional attachments. Done time and time again, the mind learns that happy is the preferred emotion which aligns your mind to "learning quiet," and then suppleness can be taught.

You know it not, there is no memory of it, but before you came into this life, you decided to come again into this physical world. You created a reason why (Life Intention Setting) and then you simply decided the where, the when, and the by whom. And so here you are. That Higher Self of you, that Higher Being that is quite literally YOU, knew that you would have thinking thoughts. They were well-prepared for it; they gave you a Guardian to help you. The Guardian

coming into this world

HS

9

Collective of Teachers

Your Guardian

is, as some of you would say, a savior, a guide, a loved one. We have much to teach you about who we are, who you are, why you are here in the physical body in a physical sub-reality, and who "guardians" your being while you are here. There is not one of you that can hear cleanly, that Higher Being, so the collective of teachers that you have while you are non-physically focused becomes your integrated set of Guides, one of which is supremely significant for this lifetime. We call your collective of teachers your Guardian and that significant Being for this lifetime your Guide.

Clairvoyant = Ocular

Many of you delightful clairvoyant (we prefer the term *ocular*) people, trance channel people, can tune into or tap into the Soul energy of another person, but not your own. It is your Guide always that you speak to but we understand that many of you mistake voices as your own Higher Self. I make this point here because there are too many mistakes made interiorly—the human mind has a capacity to hear and listen and then it absorbs what IT believes is important for your life. There is an interior mind that listens to everything that you say, think, see, hear, taste, listen to…experiences are not overlooked by the subconscious part of you.

The human mind

It takes an extremely quieted mind to hear your own Higher Being verbally—and even then, it is in small increments, yet delightful. Who do you hear, then, when ocularity is verbal? The Guardian, which is led by your Guide. Each lifetime has the same Guide. Your Higher Self speaks to you using an emotional guidance system. It is what we call the heart center, center line, or hara. The emotional guidance system are interior wavelengths that circulate at different rhythms that are understood by the human mind

Who do you hear?

EGS

EGS = the heart center, center line, hara, interior wavelengths understood as EMOTION

as an emotion.

Why emotion? Because you have learned that emotions exist, that feelings are real, that you can feel the thoughts and the intention behind them. You cannot, but to most of you, feelings and words are comingled in such a way that words themselves have meaning. Because you have emotions, we use them to speak to you, your Soul Being uses them to guide you nonverbally. That Being is the one that is participating physically with you, vested in your life and the experiences that attune to your physical being. The conduit for "communication" with that Being is the emotional guidance route, separate and distinct from the verbal, image-maker within the mind.

The Guardian is a beautiful collective of Beings that have formed together, who are not separate from you in this life but external from your own Soul Being. They speak to you through what we call the conduit, the highway, the chakratic points. They guide you, they move you, they encourage you, they love you. They have no guesswork in them. They know in every moment exactly what you are needing emotionally, intellectually, physically. Their job is purposeful. Their job is necessary. Their job IS.

The Guardian IS. Within the Guardian, there are so many lifetimes. There is no exact number because we are energy, we are intelligence, we swirl about each other, we overlap within the Guardian so that we share intelligence. We have specialties that we use. We have physical life experiences that we do *not* use. We do not impose our will on your life. We purposefully guide you based on the Life Intentions set by your Higher Being.

We move as one, but we are a collective of many. So, if you are wanting to know the name of your Guide (as many of you do), choose a name or a term that feels good to you. We are not a single lifetime. Refrain from wanting to know who your Guide is and ask instead what your life's purpose is so that you can understand what the Guide of you is here for. There is no single name to offer any of you, however, we do know how the mind works and, for some of you, IT needs to have a human name to feel secure. The reasons for this are a product of your own human experience.

For others, the mind needs to know it is real and has an awareness of the human experience when the interior mind (subconscious mind if you like the term) associates itself with the plane of existence that we are speaking from. We refrain from giving a name that is not accurate because it knows fiction if it feels it vibrationally. For those that have not learned the art of allowing, the ocular mind will not have the ability to bring forth an accurate name. There is a lack of clean, clear, accurate ability to converse with the realm of Reality and the Beings that speak with human beings. Once trained, the ocular mind can do a great many things and have accuracy that is undeniable. We want everyone to have superb abilities to speak with us, to convey information from us so that you are all instructionally guided.

When we speak through a channel, when we speak THROUGH a channel, we know that accuracy exists. The ability to channel means learning from the Guide has been accepted by the interior mind and it has learned to become soft and supple in its ability to receive, to interpret, and to translate nonverbal and verbal communication—intelligence, better said—from us. The human mind has the capacity to learn exquisite accuracy in communicating with us. It is a progression of learning that we are wanting you to recognize.

A channel is not simply an ability that some have, and some do not; it is the pinnacle ability in your world. It means that the mind has learned to trust us. It simply loves us and has decided on your behalf, to listen to lessons from us. We want all of you to learn how to be a channel. Whether you use it for monetary gain or in the public eye matters not. We want you all to have the quieted mind that is necessary *quieted mind* to be able to channel. It is the quieted mind that creates the ability to learn from the Guide. It is the supple mind that learns accuracy. It is the quiet and supple person that knows that we are Love Beings. It is the person within that we are talking about. How to become a channel is simple. Have the desire. Have the desire. Have the desire.

How do you get there? Meditation. It is the only way. It is a requirement. Not a life of solitude, although a life of gratitude. Not a life of platitudes, but a life of love and play and fun and happy. It is not always simple to put these words into action. We love you for considering these words as truth, nonetheless. We guide you to the better thought, the better example, the better ability to listen, as well as the ability to cleanly hear us.

You get to be a human being and you get to live this life fully, but we do want you to live this life knowing how to move about easier. How to manifest, because manifesting is fun. Manifesting is the reason you are here, but you are *manifest* supposed to manifest with us! How can you do that without the ability to accurately converse with us? Life is meant

13

to be happy, so manifest wealth, manifest health, manifest relationships, manifest things, manifest people, manifest experiences, manifest a new car, manifest a new house—then, de-manifest it and sell it by manifesting a buyer. Do anything that you are wanting to do. Just do not do it with hate in your heart or anger on your shoulders. Let peacefulness be the emotion that guides you.

We love you so much. Be lucky. Tell other people how lucky you are and love that you are lucky. For those of you that are looking for an explanation past lucky, well, you have come to the right place because it is what we do—we teach you. We teach you. We teach you. We teach you. We teach you how to quiet the mind. We teach you who we are. We teach you who you are, meaning this incarnated being that you are. We teach you what the world is all about, why you came here, that life includes what we call Intentions with a capital "I." We teach you how to have fun. We teach you how to remember who we are. Most importantly, we teach you how to hear us.

We want accuracy for all of you, because without it, guidance is mediocre at best. You may hear us, but the mind is subject to influence while you are receiving us ocularly. Influence creates inaccuracy, creates subjectiveness, creates confusion, creates disbelief in the ability, in general, for people to receive accurately.

At times, the mind's influence can be so concrete that the words from your Guide are not heard at all, although words themselves may be conjured. When the mind simulates conversations, it may simulate them in such a way that you believe that you are hearing your Guide. It happens far too often. It is the reason we are wanting to teach the world how to channel instead. The mind is quieter. It is a quiet and supple mind that allows. It is the quiet and supple person that behaves during meditation. It is a quiet and supple ability to receive clean, clear, and accurate time and time again.

When we teach in classroom settings; we teach you what your own Guide is doing to develop your abilities. Then we validate how you are doing. We give you not a progress report, but we do discuss your progress. We remind you what work is needed for you personally. We give you exercises; we give you homework. There are lessons. There is no requirement, however, to do them.

Channelers are clean, clear, and accurate every time because the mind does not influence the conversation. Some of you understand this and some of you do not and that is okay. This woman, Carol, she is not the one speaking, although it is her voice being recorded. We are asking the mind to stay where it is and to allow us to speak our chosen words through her. She allows us to do so.

Influence is always present until you reach the level of moving into the altered areas of the mind. Expect to be influenced but focus on it not because, if you do, the mind believes that it is supposed to do it. We want you to know that the mind WILL do it. Just pray that it does not (we tease you when we say that), but know this: it IS expected by us. It is known that the subconscious part of you will influence some part of the conversation always until you have reached the upper levels available to you (intermediate and above have less influence) it is what the mind will do. The mind in earlier levels has not learned yet to set itself aside and

15

not participate at all in the conversation.

Those of you that are a trance person, you understand this fully, that your mind simply shifts. Some of you feel it. Some of you feel motion or you feel movement or you feel energy swirling. Then you feel everything settle and the words begin out loud. It is slightly different for each human being that allows us to speak through them. We want you all to get to that point. Have fun on the way, of course, but we do want you all to get to that point, because the quieted mind hears us.

End chapter one. That is all.

CHAPTER 2

We Are Love Beings

"Your Soul Being, your Higher Self, your Expanded Being, or Soul Essence is pure—pure as the driven snow."

Session 2
Channeled April 11, 2021

Ocularity of the mind. Interior sight. We think it is a good name. Who are we? Jeshua, the Collective of Twelve. We explain now what that means. Who am I? A Being within the Jeshua Collective. I am Consciousness. I am Love. I am loving—and I am loving teaching among the Twelve. It is a level, dear one, not a number. Do understand that Twelve is a good place to be no matter who you are. I am not of Twelve, I am among them and am teaching a subject that is meaningful to you and your world.

There is this thing that you do in the world, it is called getting older. We would like to be able to say growing up, but so many of you do not. We smile when we say this, but (and truly, we do want you to have a childlike way but some of you just do not learn what you are meant to do in this life and how to do it with kindness) you do get older.

We compare it to what you do in the non-physical. We do not get older because we do not believe ourselves to be on the way to expiring. We just grow. We manifest more of ourselves. We become more. We do more. We have more experiences. We lead ourselves to water, we drink the water, and then we continue to drink the water. The water is the area of All That Is that we are wanting to explore. We are not limited to one area. We explore them all on our way to deciding what it is that we want to be a part of.

All of you wonder at one time or another why you are in the world. "What is the purpose of life?" is the all-familiar phrase. There are many reasons why your Soul Being chose to incarnate. Number one is because it was the time within your Soul Being's development to explore the world. When that time comes, you simply do it. You learn all about the worlds, what you can do in them, what has been done in them, what we do to maintain them, and then you do it. You participate in it from the outside initially.

Why do we start here, in this book? Because it is a good place to start. We teach you who we are. On the way, you learn who you are so that you can eventually learn, easily, how to open up to communication with us. So here you are as a delightful Source Being. You have developed, grown, expanded to reach the level where you have an opportunity to participate in the worlds via the manner in which you choose.

To be clear, that does mean that you have to learn all about the worlds first, what can be done and in what ways they are done. You watch it being done, learning by observation and then you learn by doing in the alternate worlds. The alternate worlds do not impact the future. We say that lightly—the future being the ongoing development of the greater part of you. The alternate worlds are practice areas. We do many of them at one time because we can do many things at one time. How many depends on how much you enjoy it.

If you enjoy it, you can do as many as you want. If that is not your favorite place to learn, you might do more or less than another Being of the same evolution. The quantity is always up to you and the practice arenas are just that, practice arenas. We do not practice how to be a person or how to stay connected to the Higher Self within a sub-reality such as the one you are reading this book from. As you learn, you progress to higher states of arenas, one of which is this sub-reality. You are in a learning environment that feels very real to you but does not have an impact on your Soul Being's ability to evolve. You are learning how to remain connected with your Higher Self but also remain in contact and communication with your Teachers.

[handwritten margin note: Earth what we are learning]

So, when your training in this area begins, you observe, you observe, you observe, and then you practice, practice, practice, practice, practice. You then have opportunities to peer into one of the earth planes, one of the concrete worlds, and see how it is done there. How what is done? Incarnating and de-carnating. It is a masterful place, a masterful place. Communicators are everywhere, although as human beings you cannot see them, but they are everywhere—some trainees and some masters of it.

A question you might ask at this point is whether it is possible to "bump into" a trainee and become frightened of Spirit Helpers, or if it possible to have a trainee as your Guide. No, we do not allow it. It is the Law of the Universes. It is a law of learning how to participate in the universes. Trainees are not able to tune into you. You are not able to tune into them. They are not Guides. They are not Spirit Helpers. They are trainees learning about the worlds. They do not and cannot affect your experience.

Some of you believe that you have Spirit around you. You are accurate. You always have Helpers influencing your actions. These are not trainees but Spirit Communicators, and the Guides, the Helpers, the experts at helping you move along this path called life. They are experts. The trainees follow the experts and watch them, and they learn. They do

21

not remove themselves from the trainee experience until they are experts at what they have chosen to learn. How do you become an expert at it? You practice. But we do not practice on people. Let that be fully understood.

There are no student Guides like a student teacher in a classroom. They observe and learn from afar, so to speak, having no influence on your human life experience. The world is not a practice field; it is observation only for the trainees. As the trainees progress, they do more things in the external worlds—the perceived environments, the alternate realities. When the trainees have reached a point in their own development in doing the specific thing that they embarked upon, then they participate in human life.

You observe and watch and learn, and then you practice, watch and learn, watch and learn, watch and learn, watch and learn, watch and learn, watch and learn. How long does it take? There is no time where we are, but time is also not of the essence. There is a curriculum that needs to be learned and you take whatever amount of "time" that is desired by you.

If participation in the worlds is a definite interest of yours, you may choose to do it quickly. If you are interested in it, but you have not come to the decision point of how you want to participate, you may do it slowly because you may be doing other things in addition to it. The possibilities are endless. The point is, we want you to understand one thing: WE DO NOT PRACTICE ON HUMAN BEINGS. There are no "oops"—ever.

The Guides, the Helpers, Communicators, the Guardian, they never "oops." They are perfect every time. They are masters of their craft. Masters of the craft. In the nonphysical dimension, mastery means perfection. Once you have reached mastery, then you become a Guide, a Helper, a Communicator, a healer, an influencer.

Some of us decide to teach because we love to teach. Some of us become human beings because that is one of the choices. So, you lovely people reading this book, look around. Every human being that you can think of, look at, have ever heard of—their Soul Being loves incarnation. Loves it. If we do not love incarnation, we would not do it. We would simply choose a different location.

We never follow the footsteps of our parents. We do have a parent, a Source of life. But we do not follow in the footsteps of that Source of life unless we choose to. We all have freedom to choose. We all have freedom to grow. We all have freedom to be. We all have freedom to become. We all have freedom to create. We all have freedom. Period. And then we just be. Forevermore.

The greater part of you is overflowing with love for this thing that you are doing (life). But at the same time, it is the greater part of you that is having this life. What you call separation, it is not real meaning; there is always connection to your Source.

This world has not aligned itself with forgiveness nor forgiving to oneself or another. But you will. How did you evolve? You simply learned to choose. You learned to make and then within the world you simply forgot that you are not the creator. You are simply making, wanting to make in the likeness of the things that your creator does. The world will forgive itself for this error, eventually. We are not worried about it, and so we do not believe that you ought to be either. We want you to love your world. We want you to know who you are. We want you to believe that the world is healthy and whole, because it is. We are Source Beings. If you continue destroying the ozone, we can replace it. We have done so before. So, worry not about it.

In this experience of worlds, you have the opportunity to choose to incarnate. You do have options. You may incarnate and try it out to have had the experience, or choose not. Or you may enter into a cycle of incarnation. It is a choice that you make ahead of time. There is no karmic reason, no karmic debt that caused you to be in the world. There is, however, life experience that may be learned and unlearned in the worlds.

We have distinct names for each choice. Angels, as we use the term, are those that have chosen to not incarnate at all or have chosen to do it less than three times to have the experience of it as part of their development. In other words, they have chosen to remain non-physically focused in their participation within the worlds. The rest have embarked upon a reincarnation cycle. It is a cycle. Each one of you decide what it is that you are wanting out of that particular cycle and then you do it.

You plan to experience a great many things during each incarnation experience, some things you specifically choose to not include. It is a plan that you have, a personal curriculum built during your trainee experiences. As you experience physical life, you begin making choices on what to include in successive lives and what to learn within the realm of existence that we refer to as the Reality of Consciousness.

The ideas for your physical life are what we are talking about here—what you are wanting to include, learn, experience, take part in, and be a part of. The ones you personally want to have become your Life Intentions. Interesting fact is that your Intentions have everything to do with the growth, the expansion, the upward ascension of your own Soul Being, and in that way aids the expansion of All That Is.

Your own expansion is why you are here. You have your own Intentions for coming here, meaning physical incarnation. There are things that your Soul Being wants you to do or figure out or learn or undo. That is a reading that every one of you ought to have: "What are the Intentions of my Soul Being that are meaningful for me to know in this point in my life?" That would be the best topic for a reading, it is the best information ever, so you know where you are meant to be, who you are meant to become. Follow-up sessions on where you go from here to provide continual verbal guidance. Substitute instructions for that is what it is.

You are not pawns that get moved and shoved about— go do this, go do that, based on these Life Intentions. The objectives are much broader: "I want to experience life from a different perspective. I want to slow down in this life and appreciate more. I want to undo an angry thread that I experienced in a few lifetimes now and I want to work out the kinks, so to speak." Worry not about how to involve yourself in the process of discovering the methods or actions to accomplish your Intentions, however, because your heavenly being draws experiences to you so that they can have an opportunity to do just that.

As human beings, you just have a way of waking up

negative
Belief

Soul
Intention

Behaviors

every day, living life blindly, meaning emotionally, going to sleep, and doing it again, day after day, after day, after day, after day. Because of that, you create beliefs—negative ones—that make it difficult for your Higher Self to maneuver you through life, to be able to do or learn or have or be the thing that they were hoping for. Hence, the <u>need</u> for information on Soul Intentions for this life to get you back on track, to help you understand why a particular pattern of behavior may be present. Sometimes a behavior is "built-in," but often you acquired it. When the latter is the case, it is always greatly desired that you rid your life of it, and we get to work to help you.

We are helping you all the while, but much, if not most, of it goes unnoticed. When you understand what the Guide is doing and why, it allows some of you to accept life easier, you just roll with it. "So, I'm supposed to make a left turn? Because I would have made a right turn." And we say, "Left turn, please." The human being that says, "Okay, left turn it is," and then starts to see evidence of alignment with their Soul Intentions. How do you know an experience is a Soul Intention? You do not. It is not necessary that you do, however, some experiences that are in alignment with them will cause you great joy, or perhaps great acclaim if that is something that your Intentions included.

For example, the "anger thread" Intention. Alright, this is a good example for a great many of you. So, if a Soul Being has an Intention to rid its incarnation experience (to remove anger), there will be an opposing effect, or an additional emotional thread included so that the human being finds/allows balance. As an example, you may add curiosity in spades so anger fades quickly, or you may add a deep abiding love for the elderly, which causes you to have a strong association with your grandmother and by doing so you learn gentle ways alongside having a temper.

The hope from your Higher Being is that you choose to favor gentility over anger. There are many examples, and none are meant to cause you to become angry. You always have another aspect or Intention built in to supplement or increase your ability to learn what you were hoping to. Life does not always afford you an easy opportunity to see life from alternate viewpoints. It is one of the reasons for this book and others like it.

There is a need to pause here and explain some things for those that have not received our teachings before. Soul Being is a term that we use because the world uses it, or some words like it. We enjoy teaching all of you and we find that some of you enjoy teaching as though you are us and then the world gets confused because, we love you so much, but people do not understand the Conscious realm of Reality. Your Soul Being, your Higher Self, your Expanded Being, or Soul Essence is pure—pure as the driven snow. It is fluid love, parched never; human tendencies do not exist where Love Beings are from. Where Reality IS.

We experience physical sub-reality life as a means to expand All That Is. As a means of evolving our own Being. What we are is alive, intelligence walking. We are profoundly gifted in all things. All of us. That includes the greater Being that is your Higher Self. You are not in the physical world because you are incapable of evolving. You are here simply because it is your learning experience to do so.

27

Life here in the physical world includes sub-reality consciousness and Reality consciousness. Sub-reality consciousness is a fancy term for energy body which is your Soul Essence. It contains life experiences of YOU (in the physical worlds, anyway). This is purity. This is love. This is creation. This is you. The You where we are dictating this work from is all-encompassing, ever-expanding, liquid love. And intelligence. We are fluid, evolving yet evolved Beings that have no emotional state below love. Except that we do when we are having an incarnated experience. It is this experience that gets contaminated then purified during the Transition. It is this energy body that we use again and again. It is the energy body filtering that is conducted during each successive life. It is fun for us to explain it in this depth of detail.

Your emotions are harsh in this world that you are experiencing. They are not desired, nor are they bad exactly. They allow your Higher Self to choose what to include in another lifetime. They use life experience as an array of options and your life adds to the mix. It adds flavor to the recipe, a little of this, a little of that—and once in a while too much of this or too much of that. It does not spoil the dish, it simply means we begin adding a little more of something else to balance the overall flavor.

We nonphysical vibrational beings cannot, will not, ever have an emotional state that is less than purity of love. So, in the incarnated state, if a Soul Being has had a single lifetime, or many lifetimes, where anger has been a problem based on life experience—you still get to do what you want to do. Free will, it is a law of this experience called incarnating.

Free will brings to All That Is, newness, expansion.

So, back to the story. Soul Being "A" has had five lifetimes where they were incapable of choosing the better thought and thereby selecting joy over anger. Perhaps they were raised by parents who had too little money or too much and were egotistical and portrayed themselves as being "better than." The child watched the parents behave this way and followed suit or rebelled because it did not seem right. Again, the possibilities are endless. He/she may have rebelled so much that they found themselves engaged to someone who smacked them around a bit. Then they became not only angry but afraid of every little thing.

The Soul Being is wanting so much for that human being to step away from that experience and go back to the last place that felt good, the last place that felt secure, that last place they felt safe physically, mentally, and emotionally. This is a page to be underlined and dog-eared, for sure. Go back to the place of feeling good—physically or even in your mind. It will help you so very much in this lifetime, as well as in all others, because you will have learned how to do it. Then you can reach back into the history books, so to speak, and borrow that knowledge in a future life and use it.

So, here is this Soul Being who has had several incarnated experiences where anger has been a problem and not resolved or not resolved enough. They embark upon a lifetime where the Soul Being says, "This is the lifetime where I'm going to focus on recuperating from anger." What does that mean for your life if you are the human being that is the manifestation of the Being who wanted this Intention included in the next lifetime?

Well, anything. You could be picked on. You might have the bad, mean teacher. You could have the car that breaks down a lot. You could have mechanical things, we will say, that do not go right for you. You could have not enough money, or much money but no friends to do things with. Anger could creep in and rear its ugly head from anywhere. But in that type of incarnated experience, the "ugly anger head" will present itself, as well as the opposing Intentions. They are always both present.

Why do some of you have anger and some of you do not? Well, for some of you, you are working on it. It is an Intention for you to experience it so that you may rid yourself of it. Is that mean? No. It just is. We decide to do something, we follow through with it. But we do not leave you out in the cold by yourself. It is why you have this emotional guidance system; it is why you have this beautiful collective of Beings we call The Guardian and the head honcho we call a Guide. It is why you have Spirit Communicators everywhere to help you think the better thought, see the better thing, remember some other experience, to distract you long enough to choose better.

If you are reading this book, you have been guided to it—to the subject matter, for sure. Even if you are hating this book or understand none of it, you have been guided to it because it might be the thing that is opening you up to truth, and thereby (using the anger experience) to rid, or walk away from, anger.

The examples are so many. The anger thread is but one that we talk about in this moment. Intentions are never single, so do not misunderstand that a Soul Being would have an

Intention to have a life full of anger. That is not the case. Nor do we say that a lifetime has to be full of anger. You can perceive anger and because of life experience, people in your life, books that you read, the shows that you chose instead of something else, might have enough to be able to step away from anger. You might have recognized that being kinder to yourself felt better and then you choose it more often. You might have gotten the mean teacher but noticed the kind lunch lady and decided internally to emulate her, for example, and that might be enough.

Do not believe that an emotional Intention from a Soul Being means that you have a "ball and chain." You do not have one. You can cut the cord of that emotional tie and be done with it the first time it shows up in your life and then fill your life with alternate experiences. Choose what to see in this world of yours. Choose wisely what to see. Some experiences will feel good and some will not. You could rid yourself of anger and find yourself filled with conceit instead. Well, if this is the case then you simply have something else to play with either in this lifetime or another and then your Guide has something else they get to help you with—externally, meaning in the perceived environments or in another incarnation experience.

This is a playground. That is what we are wanting you to fully understand. It is a playground. This thing called Earth, this thing called life in a human body, is a playground where you get to be the one playing while you are in physical body. When you are not in a physical body, you are helping those that are. Every single time. Every single time. Every single time.

It is what we all do. We either "people-ize" ourselves, or we help those that have focused themselves into the world and into physical form. We guide you. We love you. We communicate with you. We protect you. We talk to you. We surround you. We teach you. We help you in ways that you are not aware of, most of you.

Most of you are not hyper-aware that we are around, guiding you. But, when you become one of those hyper-aware people, you cannot help but love it because you see us everywhere. You see us helping you everywhere. You see yourself manifesting things left and right. Life just gets better and better. Knowing a little bit about how you acquired this thing called a human body is helpful in giving you the foundation necessary to fully understand that communicating with your nonphysical counterparts is built in.

The Guardian is a collective of Beings who bring together all of the knowledge necessary to keep you physically focused—meaning the Soul Being of you, to keep the Soul Being of you physically focused in the world. They are a Helper to your Soul Being on remaining in the physical world. It is a partnership, while also guiding you in this lifetime.

Spirit Communicators are those Beings who are currently not in physical form. They are Conscious Beings that assist when asked by Guides to nudge or help you maneuver should you not make a meaningful decision by yourself. They do many things. For instance, you leave your house intending to go across town to your favorite store, and come home. Part-way through that journey, you remember that you needed to pick up some milk. You look down and you have your wallet with you, and you look at the clock and you say to yourself, "I believe I have enough time, lucky me." So, you put your car in reverse, and you zip or skedaddle over to another store, and you pick up your milk and you get home. Later that evening, you go to make dinner that included scalloped potatoes—of which milk is one of the required ingredients.

You think you simply remembered something, call it a coincidence. We say you heard something from a Spirit Communicator. It is called an intuited thought, a received thought, a spirit nudge—assistance. Spirit Communicators help you in your day-to-day life. Why do you sometimes forget things then? Because your minds are active organisms that are sometimes too busy to hear your friendly spirit crew.

Spirit Communicators/Helpers are not the only ones forging your way. The Guardian is also doing that, and the entire birth Collective, at the request of the Guide. Although the Guardian Collective is helping to keep you in the physical sub-reality, they are not so busy as to not know what you are needing every moment of every day. Spirit Communicators do not do the things that your Guide has overlooked, they are responding to requests from that powerful Being.

They are helping your Soul Being to have each life Intention satisfied and simultaneously taking care of many physical things for you. They teach your mind how to be quiet and how to regulate your emotions. They bring forth experiences for you to recall and show them to you in the mind's eye. You call it a memory, many of which—most of which—are meant to guide you into a better-feeling thought.

Law of Attraction, however, is. Period. It is always at

Soul Being = you

play. It is the opposite of life in the Conscious Reality. Everyone from the nonphysical dimension is working overtime to help shift your gaze to something that feels better, using memories, people, activities, almost anything that does or might interest you.

Spirit Communicators can be Beings who are still involved in the reincarnation cycle, but are in-between lives. Or, they may be finished with the cycle and have decided to do something different and remain non-physically focused.

We use the term Spirit Communicator rather than the more frequent, overused term Guide here because it simply is not accurate enough. Spirit Communicators communicate to many. Spirit Communicators help many. The Guide is always focused on you and your life. The Soul Being is the one having your life. The terminology is fun, is it not? We will emphasize this—there are many terms that the world uses. We consistently use the plethora of your phrases so that no matter what your background or foundation is, your mind will rest easy knowing it has learned where to place your vernacular in the collective Knowing of how the worlds work.

So, who are we as the Jeshua Collective? We are teachers and healers who have learned all there is to know about the worlds, living in them, acquiring them, maintaining them, healing them, catapulting them into another dimension and so we have completed our learning on them, so to speak. Some call us Ascended, Ancient Ones, The Brethren. We say, learned in all things. We step in at different phases in your life experience to help advance you along your Intended path. Not because your Guide is not capable of assisting you

34

but because it was built-in that we intervene if and when your life evolved in the correct pathways.

When you start to understand who you are in the non-physical dimension, life does not seem quite as hard and this is why; when you find out that you chose to be a human being, that you do this thing continuously and that there are Intentions identified for you and by you, and that you do have Guides and Communicators and you do have a bunch of us helping you, you do not feel quite as alone. You begin to realize, hopefully, that manifesting a life that feels good to you is a lot easier than you have made it out to be.

Ask it of us and we give it to you. Ask it of us and we give it to you. Ask it of us and we give it to you. If there is no resistance, no energy blocks, then you receive it immediately.

How do you know if you have resistance? Negative emotion is present, doubt being a substantial factor in this particular world. Your Guide is always moving energy around your body, within your body, and examining your thoughts to help create a better situational awareness within you. All of you fight the urge to be nicer and you all have substantial guilt. It is not guilt that the Guide offers you but a better feeling, which in the moment of doubt could cause you to feel anxiety or hopeful. Why does your mind choose one over the other? Patterns of behavior seen, experienced, heard.

Choose wisely what to pay attention to and the emotional guidance received by your Higher Being and your Guide. It is the job of your Guide to create with you. Follow emotional guidance and choose the better thought and manifesting a life of easy experiences will be found, time and time again. It is their job to create for you, based on what you have asked for—Soul Intentions and human intentions. When you hear them, your wish list gets answered faster.

You make everything that you have in your life. You have manifested it based on what you focus on, what you think you are going to get—some of which is forward-thinking, and you have this uplifted view of what you could have. All of you also use your own personal, private, experiential life to tell you what you cannot have.

This attractor within, The Law (because it is the most important law within this physical sub-reality), is free will. It is how your current evolution of man has evolved itself into the separation or the belief of it. Choice. You have a choice. Choice to know who you are and ignore it or choice to believe in what this book is telling you. You have a choice to ask, or you have a choice to go it alone.

You are not alone; we are always helping you. Co-creating is the primary job of the those of us who are not physically focused, but you are not aware of it nor aware of the instructions coming to you. You have Communicators with you nearly every minute of every day and a Guide with you every microsecond. You have a Higher Self, a Soul Being that decided to have you and guides you emotionally alongside your Guide and just as frequently. You have those of us that have ascended fully to call upon. You have emotional indicators to help you to know whether you are resisting assistance or allowing us to help you.

Why do we start here? Because it is the perfect place to start. You are beginning to hear us, on the inside. The egoic self is beginning to listen to the words. We guide your ability to hear us by the words written page by page. Do not concern yourself with perfection, with understanding the levels, the terms, the whys and the why-nots. We are structuring this book to open your mind to allow us to integrate with your lives. To see us not, but to hear us vibrationally. Meditation is key. Meditation is always the best place to learn to have quiet conversations with us. We will continue along this thread throughout each chapter.

All is well. That is all for this chapter.

Soul Being

Higher Self

Expanded Being

Soul Essence

the greater part of you

your parent being

the you - not - you

in the nonphysical

the ocean of you

CHAPTER 3

The Essential Material Introduced

"Energy is not constant.
We are electromagnetic energy Beings.
It is the best description."

Session 3
Channeled April 11, 2021

We are going to focus a little bit more on who you are and what we call Intentions. Intentions are something that we think up. We, that Soul Being that is that greater part of you, that parent being, the you-not-you in the nonphysical, that ocean of you. We have so many beautiful descriptions for who that Being is. That Being designs not your life, end-to-end, moment by moment, for it is not a life full of manipulated experiences. It is a life of Intended pathways to learning more about being a human being. That is where the Intentions come in.

We do not have prescribed curricula for our life experiences. We shall call them incarnations primarily. We are not carbon copies of each other and therefore do not set about to learn the exact same things. We do not all have the same Intentions for a single lifetime nor an entire cycle. Although, the cycles overall do aid your learning.

There is no deviation once you have set yourself on the path of a cycle. You do it once. Everybody, everybody, everybody learns everything about the worlds. Once you do, you then have an opportunity to experience life once or twice before you make a decision on whether or not you will participate in a cycle. That is why we said less than three. We are all Angelic Beings. We use the term Angel versus Spirit Being to help you understand the process your Higher Self is taking to determine how to evolve. If you are a person, they are either pursing a cycle or experiencing life for the Choice. In either case, it is purposeful and full of purposes.

41

Does everybody have to be a person at least one time? Yes. We have not expressed the details like this before. Some of you will be asking insightful questions so we are giving you a preface of information. Do not dissect the information to acquire knowledge for it is all but a part of the whole. Do not subject yourself to internal personal criticism should the material seem daunting or "above your head." It is not intended that you conclude each page with doubt or self-deprecation. It is intended that you read slowly, digesting at a pace that feels good to you.

Should you read quickly you will want to come back to a page sooner or later to learn the material deeper. Do dog-ear, do write in the margins, do make annotations. Do learn as you go but, dear ones, do not analyze and harm yourself with doubt that this life is as we say. It is for you to decide what to learn, here in this physical place. It is for your Higher Being to see through your experiences to what is necessary to evolve.

It is in conjunction with the Guide—substitute Teacher, for that is who the Guide is for each of you—that decisions are made. What kind of decisions? All of them. But you know it not. Very few of you hear us and even less hear us accurately. We are intently interested in correcting this and becoming the Beings that you seek out to learn how to communicate with us, your Teachers, your Loved Ones, your Relatives, and those "beyond the grave," for those that prefer that way of thinking.

Who is writing this chapter? Another Being withing the Jeshua Collective. I have taught through human beings before but I am teaching a different set of subjects through this

Carol - Channel

new channel. She likes to say she is the conduit for Source knowledge to flow. I think that is an apt way at looking at her abilities.

Ocularity of the mind is the material that I am teaching now. I announce myself at this point simply because I choose to. I am an entity. I am a teacher. I am an Ascended one. I am one of those Twelve. I have mastered the worlds—more or less now, there are still worlds that I have not encountered, however I do not intend to encounter them for they are not in my Intended path. When we say we have learned everything there is to know, it is so but the caveat is that "everything" includes all there is to know about the world and those like it that you are currently experiencing.

My Higher Self is aware of this conversation, and they do experience life from an even higher perspective and as such teach in other realms of existence. I have not yet come to those experiences and am not fully immersing myself in them as of yet. I will earmark this page for myself in the akashic, for I like the memory of writing it. As I have said, I am among the Jeshua Collective. How many lifetimes have I had? A lot. Why do I not use a name? Because it is not necessary, it will detract from the message because there are so many obstinate people in your world. That is unfortunate, but not all is lost. My teaching will continue.

As a Collective, we are teaching on subjects that have a basis in All That Is. We call it The Essential Material. Pillar 1; The Foundational Material about Conscious Beings; Pillar 2; Law of Personal Reality; Pillar 3; Self-Healing; and Pillar 4; Intuitive Development. We enjoy these subjects very much and, if I do say so myself, the suite of Beings

The Essential Material

that have identified themselves as the Jeshua Collective are pleased to present The Essential Material through a single channel. She has softened her mind well.

Everything has a boundary, even the teaching from this realm that I am speaking from. We liken it to curriculum. It is a necessary component of evolution on this planet and others like it. It is happy/sad that I am here again. Why is this, you might ask. Because I am not able to sit and write it myself. I have been working with Carol's High Guide to create in her the ability to auto-type. I have a great fondness for voice texting! It is fun, is it not, to capture thoughts in the moment? I agree.

"Intuitive Studies" is the generic term for what I teach here. I am among the Jeshua Collective. We teach as one but I am writing this chapter as an individual entity. The Jeshua Collective does not have lifetimes to point back to as I do, The Jeshua Collective is a name that was chosen not by this girl (our endearing name for her) but by us as a Collective.

Why did we choose that name? Because it refers to the full breadth of teaching that the one you know of as Jeshua (in human form) taught the world. We believe it is an apt title. With it we expand the world's view of Jeshua (the person) and we also are setting ourselves up for explaining how a Collective is formed and why and when we use it. It aids your development, in other words.

Unfoldment into channeling is the ultimate level at which we want to take you. What does Unfoldment include? Intuition, ocular-vibrational receiving, and channeling. Ocularity of the mind is one segment of a larger body of knowledge—The Essential Material.

Why do I step forward to teach this subject? Because it was my agreement with Carol's Soul Being. It was a dual Intention between us so I may continue teaching in the world. I channel individually through many. If you enjoy my chapter then ask it of me specifically, to help you understand the material. I take great care in your development as I want the world to hear us clearly.

There are many entities that have reached the "teacher of the teacher" level. Are we the highest level that there is? No. Should you be reaching higher than this level for the most complete answer? No. Are we qualified or good enough to explain to you how to communicate with us? Yes! It is what we do, what we have done for millenniums. At this level Twelve, we teach. We are the highest-level Beings that interact with your world and others like it. I enjoy my job as a teacher very much.

Energy is not constant. We are electromagnetic energy Beings. It is the best description. Energy does not die, and because it does not die, it is not constant. So, these things that you can hold or pick up, these building blocks, the literal kind, there is movement within. Science has identified some movement within. Consciousness is. Period.

Ocularity of the mind is but one segment of learning to channel. I am pleased to teach you this new subject.

That is all. Chapter is complete.

CHAPTER 4

Left – Right – Center

"Your life is a continuous stream of, innocuous though it seems, reality. Your mind, the depths of it, creates your reality. Everything you do, you have created. Everything you have, you have manifested."

Session 4
Channeled April 11, 2021

Alright. Here we go. It is a little chilly outside. What is today? It is April 11, 2021 and it is 4:05 in the afternoon. Carol is getting all situated. She is hiccupping and drinking Perrier with lime, has a peanut butter-slathered granola bar in the belly, along with some chocolate Zingers. She is hungry. She does not know why.

She wants some food. Again, she does not know why. She is not hungry, meaning the belly is not gurgling, making noises to indicate hunger but the interior part of her is wanting food. In fact her exterior desire for food (hunger) was satisfactorily satiated with the Zinger, however the inner part of her is still hungry. She does not know it. She is not feeling hungry exteriorly any longer.

Who said when the belly is gurgling, it means you are hungry? Somebody. And now, when the belly makes a noise, people say, "Oh, you must be hungry," and then they find themselves eating. She is not that kind of hungry. There are no gurgling noises in the belly but yet she is desiring food. Again, she does not know why.

There was a delightful conversation that we just had after several hours doing video dictation for this book. She/ We paused, ran over to Home Depot to grab some cans of paint and on the way we told her not to dilly-dally because she/we have things to do. In her usual flippy way, she said, "Okay." Delightful that she just says, okay.

After she said okay, on the inner part of her there was a portion that said, "Ah, but I might go shopping. I need to get some plants." So, there she was. She puts her order in at the paint counter and then she pushed the cart all the way out to where the plants are. She looked around but did not see what she wanted. She goes in the outdoor area to see if there was something there that interested her, floats around a little bit, eyes something that she likes but it was not quite right for her home.

She gets her paint and hops in the car. It is only a mile from here to home. On the way there, she says to us, "I really just want chocolate." It was our turn to say okay. Then she stopped because we are having these video sessions and she is learning the material and asked, "Does my body want chocolate?" We said, "Yes, it does." She said, "Okay." Then she continued and said, "Does my...is my body telling me to eat chocolate or does my body want chocolate?" In all fairness, she does know a thing or two about unconscious beliefs, but it was the first time that she asked a question in that way. There is an interesting point here—we will finish the story first.

We said, "In this case, just get chocolate, it feels good." She said, "Okay. I do know I only want a little bit but I do not know what kind of chocolate I want"—and then, boom! A picture of a Reese's peanut butter egg shows up in her mind. She says, "Oh! That will be delightful. Just one."

We began to say something to her but stopped because her mind went on to what she was doing. Her focus went from conversing with us to paying attention to driving. That is how interior conversations are with her. They are ongoing conversations—companions we are with her. When a conversation stops, we pick it up where we left off if the need is still present. All minds do what hers did.

So here she is, driving, and decides to turn into Rite-Aid, full intention on grabbing one Reese's peanut butter egg, leave her fifty cents on the counter and go out the door. But then she sees a red coconut Zinger. They are one of her favorites. She does not know why. The other day, we said, "Carol, you like coconut." She has had enough of these conversations with us that the old questions do not come forward anymore, and she said, "Oh! I get it, I like-like coconut" (meaning there is a belief in her that coconut is good). We said, "Yes, you do and it is always something you are happy to eat."

At that moment, her father said, "I liked chocolate as well," because in her mind she was putting coconut and chocolate together. Carol and her father shared enjoyment of this thing called an Almond Joy; they both really liked chocolate. The father like-liked chocolate. Carol does too, and she like-likes coconut. Her father (during his life) examined coconut and agreed that it went with chocolate. Carol examined coconut and decided she likes it.

Unconscious beliefs are resident in the world. We want to undo a great many of them—I like it, I like it not. I like it, I like it not—it just, is. Then sometimes you come upon those things that we call "treasures," true preferences. Coconut is a true preference of Carol.

Okay. She and her father both have a true preference of milk chocolate. The father had a life experience where chocolate and coconut seemed to do well together. It is the interior mind that we are referring to. Carol's interior mind prefers both, individually as well as together. It like-likes chocolate and like-likes coconut. The father simply like-liked chocolate. Are you getting this? We hope so.

This is important because as we are walking into Rite-Aid, she sees the dessert that she loves (coconut Zinger). But in that moment, she looked up and selected something that she rarely chooses, a chocolate Zinger. Recognizing the sudden change in her selection, she said to us, "I'm just going with it, it looks good."

So here she is, buying this package of chocolate Zingers, knowing that it is an unusual choice. She opens it up on the way out of Rite-Aid and the first reaction on the taste buds are mediocre. Instead of throwing it away she said to us that she was going to continue eating it. She just wanted chocolate, remember? We replied, "Well done" and then had the conversation about the emotional guidance system and that her body wanted the chocolate. It mattered not if she was pleased with it.

That is how it is for all of you. You pass through emotional guidance so quickly. We give you this anecdote because even those with strength in their ocular abilities overlook emotional guidance.

Interestingly, the chocolate did not satiate her hunger. The belly, again, is not rumbling but she feels like it is time to eat. She has not had an actual meal—and there is the answer to the internal hunger. What she had eaten earlier registered in her as snacking but what she really desired was a meal.

So here we go again, another example. On the inside, we call it preference, Carol likes her homemade lattes the best. It is an internal decision that hers are preferred. However, she does like to frequent Starbucks even though she likes theirs least. Why does she go? Because she likes the app on her phone. Why does she like the app? Because it is something that she can do easily. She likes racking up the points and getting something for free. She also adds money quickly, there is less decision-making that goes into it.

In other words, she has less time to second-guess herself. Nor does she think about how much she spends on coffee when using the app, it has become fun to add and purchase, add and purchase. Internally, she also likes that the app always works—there is no resistance in using it. In addition, there is always favoritism. For her, a favoritism cropped up on Alexandria where she found a delightful Starbucks and other favorites—stone foundation, "old timey", wooden ceiling beams, and curbs on the edge of cobblestone sidewalks.

She likes to say that she does not like coffee, she likes the aroma, but masks it with syrup. "I don't drink coffee" she says, "I drink lattes." But why does she drink coffee at all? There are many reasons: it is an adult thing to do, it is fun, and her parents drank coffee daily are the biggest ones.

For these lattes that she drinks for the experience, she generally uses almond milk. Coconut milk and almond milk—truly, they have a fraction of a difference in flavor, but she would be better off ordering coconut milk because of these two things: number one she prefers (internal preference, as we have mentioned) coconut in general, and number two, later in life she "acquired an allergy" to almonds. A little tickle in the throat is what she sometimes felt. As she thinks, the body does.

Until energy work, that is. She can now put a dribble of almond extract in her coffee, use almond milk, or gobble up a handful of almonds without a tickle in the throat. How does she do that? Well, that is energy work, but the coconut milk, she would do better digesting it, because of the true preference; the treasure is coconut, not almond. The body will always prefer (do better with) coconut if given the choice. How does the mind receive a choice when she ritually orders almond milk? It sees the menu.

You may not realize it yet, but before the end of this book—or perhaps this chapter—you will hopefully understand that the eyes themselves see everything, even those things that go unnoticed by your consciously-aware mind. So, coconut will always behave better in her body when her mind is aware of the choice.

In what way do true preferences and favoritism manifest? Typically, she does not finish the coffee, or she does not always have time to stop at Starbucks, or (as is the case in this new location in Pittsburgh) she keeps forgetting where Starbucks is. It appears to be a memory problem. It is not, we assure you. It is a preference that is not satiated. Why not satiated? Because she longs for Alexandria (in general) but also the Starbucks she prefers—we will enhance this and say "internally loved." She loves that Starbucks and the body prefers that one. So it bypasses the knowing of those that are nearby in her new location.

That is the Law of Attraction. You think, therefore you are. You experience and therefore you are.

Your life is a continuous stream of, innocuous though it seems, reality. Your mind, the depths of it, creates your reality. Everything you do, you have created. Everything you have, you have manifested. Do you have a forgetful mind?

54

A Lexus? A desire for coconut or a piece of chocolate in that moment? A sore foot? An eyelash that keeps bothering you? A dishwasher that never cleans properly? Shoes that are too loose?

A driver's license from Virginia sits in her wallet, although she has lived here in Pittsburgh for three months. She has time to do all kinds of things but why not re-register the car and get the proper I.D.? Because she likes Alexandria better. The mind likes Alexandria better. The depths of the mind. She likes both, although she knows it not. She has not been here long enough for things to begin manifesting, to show her that she also likes this new place.

When we look at her, we can see all the way into the pattern of her life, and we can dissect it and we can review it, analyze it not, we just know the patterns. We look at it and we say, "Yes, that is a preference. Yes, that too is preference, as well as that one. And then we also see up-coming preferences that have not yet registered within the inter-mind. We see all.

Evidence of enjoying this new location will manifest unless she focuses on the differences between this place and Alexandria. She was doing just that daily and we told her that she needs to love this place—to love on this place. We asked her to go for a drive with us—truly, we said, "Get in the car, Carol. Let's go for a drive." We drove the hills and we drove the back roads, the highways, the neighborhoods, and she started to find her way around. We pointed out some things and drove back into her community. All of this was to help her learn to love on this new location.

Where she sits here on her balcony, she is fifty feet from

a coffee shop. A coffee shop in the center of her neighborhood is one of the things that registered in her mind as a Desire, capital D, which came about on a trip to Ocean City, Maryland with her now-defunct relationship (that, we are happy about). Better said, her Higher Self is appreciative that she is no longer in that relationship. Why? Because her abilities to communicate with us, we say gift to us, would not have manifested.

Did we have a hand in the breakup? Yes, we sure did. It was emotionally unhealthy, unstable, and she was suffering daily. We always help you. Does it seem strange for us to be happy when you are no longer suffering? We hope not. Nonetheless, why would we have a hand in two people dissolving a relationship? Because you people choose the wrong partners, or you stay with a person far longer than was necessary.

This world is a place of learning. Start looking at it that way and you will do yourself a favor. You will move quickly through experiences and not attach yourself to the emotional memory of that situation. Instead, you will gravitate towards the next one and the next, and the next. You will delight in it, or at least learn to accentuate the positive on your way to becoming happy with the ability to gravitate easier to the next person or experience.

Emotional attachments are not good in general and certainly unhelpful in learning your ocular abilities. It causes things like overeating, gallbladder removal, pancreatic cancer, left hip bursitis, being the one person at a picnic who gets stung by a bee…. There are so many variations it is, quite literally endless. It is Law of Attraction. The interior

Emotional attachment

56

mind acts like a radar and it absorbs and draws data and spits it back at you in this thing called life.

Life includes thoughts, memories, negative emotion. Balance feels like calm—emotional balance, it feels like calm. We like to say it feels regular, feels like nothing, feels normal. Upset, however, feels bad. Happy, on the other hand, is an emphatic regular, positive – positive.

Balance

When you have an experience that enhances neutral, it feels good. When you have an experience that detracts from neutral, it feels bad. In that way, the mind gives you its preference. A bit of semantics, but not that much. The mind has preferences, but those preferences are based on your reality.

You, the human being, whatever you look at, whatever you taste, whatever you engage in, whatever you ingest mentally or physically, the mind experiences. When you focus on things for longer and longer and longer periods of time, it accumulates no resistance to it. Inoculation.

At the same time, it is not unaware of quantity. Quantity wins. Those things that are high in quantity get attention and it brings more like it to you. Those things that do not have a lot of quantity, but have no emotional resistance, meaning no similar experience that was negative, is what we describe as secondary preference. Quantity always comes first. Less quantity, yet positive only, comes second. Less quantity, negative emotional variant, comes third.

The problem is that the human mind has a tendency to overlook happy because it registers it as neutral. You experience something and you enjoy it. Joy is an expectation of the mind and so an infrequent occurrence barely registers

Joy

57

as an event. Very happy registers. Unhappy to any degree, registers. That is why, my dear friends, negative events seem to be more prevalent, but they are not.

However, if we were looking solely at quantity, positive wins out every single time for all of you. When you add emotion to the occurrence, then it is "registered" or "barely registered." It is either on the map (registered) or touching the map (barely registered). It is a good description. So, when you say it is hard to get over something, we say it is, but it is not. It is not hard to find something else to look at and enjoy. But the capacity of the mind tells you that it cannot find a happy feeling because in that moment it is not looking at the edge of the map, it is looking smack-dab in the middle of the map. You have to train the mind to look for the positive—to look for the edge of the map.

We want all of you to take a page out of any notebook, carry it with you every day and spend five minutes sitting and looking about wherever you are, traffic jams included, and write down every positive aspect about it. "I love that it's Tuesday, I love 2:00. 2:00 is my favorite time of day. I love how many different cars there are. I love that some have one person, and some have two. I love bumper stickers. I love how many bumper stickers I can see from sitting right here. I love that I can turn the music on or off. I love that I can pop my earbuds in. I love that I have earbuds. I love that I can put one bud in an ear and not the other. I love that I can open my window. I love that I can open my window with the touch of a button. I also love the crank opener because I remember being a child and having one and I like memories. I love memories. Memories are good. I think I am making a memory right now and I think it is a happy one. I love this day. I am so happy that I am in a traffic jam. So funny. Traffic jam. I love...jam. I love jam. I think I love jam the best. I love that strawberry jam has chunks of strawberries. I love strawberry jam. I love raspberry jam. I think I might love blueberry jam or boysenberry jam. Any kind of jam is my favorite and I love it on toast. I love it when toast is just golden brown, but I love it on toast. I also love it with peanut butter..."

Five minutes a day for thirty days is all it takes to retrain the mind to look at the edge of the map, meaning to look for the positive. Then, when you are in a bad mood it will not be so difficult to pull yourself out of it.

Many of you do positive aspect training, mindfulness techniques. You do not do it near enough and you are not consistent enough. You do it when you are having a bad day, but you do not do it on purpose to retrain the mind. But do, do it. One sheet of paper, once a day for one five-minute segment with one intention for it—to retrain the mind to find neutral and/or neutral-plus, meaning positive.

When you do, you will be one of those people that says, "I get out of a bad mood easy. I am rarely in a bad mood, actually. I think I am hardly ever in a bad mood. You know, I barely even know anybody that is in a bad mood. I do not think I have anybody around me that is even frequently in a bad mood."

In later stages, you say things like, "I cannot remember the last time I was around an argument." Not in it, around it because it is nowhere to be found in your experience. Everywhere you go, people are happy. Everywhere you go, people are having fun. Everywhere you go, people are getting along. Everywhere you go, people are enjoying themselves—including you!

How does that happen? Because, when you retrain the mind to find happy, it does. It could be that the experiences that you are having truly do not have any sad faces, or the mind keeps your face looking left if the sad face is over on the right and in that way you do not see it. So, it might as well not even be there.

Whatever you focus on, you get more of. Whatever you love upon, you get faster. Love this activity and the positive effects will happen in thirty days. That one is an absolute because it is how long it takes the human mind, regardless of who you are. It takes thirty days back-to-back, mind you, of this exercise to retrain the mind to begin to search on its own for neutral or neutral-plus. (positive)

If, in addition to this, you incorporate "lightness of words"; meditation; listen to songs that feel good; watch comedies instead of gore; draw, color, or engage in an artistic endeavor; skip television in general; grow your own vegetables instead of reaching into the freezer or the pantry; talk over the phone instead of text—there will be a more positive impact on your inner mind.

Let's say that you believe you are shy, and because of that you desire to text instead of call. Force yourself to call because you will become less shy. At the very least, you might make a friend, or have a better conversation. But afterwards, if you beat up on yourself and you say, "I probably sounded dumb. I don't like calling people. I can't stand my voice. I got tongue-tied. That was just awful. I never want to do that again." Well, then you not only did not capitalize on the opportunity to find neutral or neutral-plus but you will be at neutral-minus.

You cancel out positive intention when it's followed by negative self-talk. It is not "plus fifty, minus fifty." It is always "plus fifty, minus fifty-one," because negativity is what you left the mind to focus on. Then negative emotion registers in the mind as something to pay attention to. Positive emotion that gets registered as something to pay attention to has more weight. There is no variation to this. So end on positive notes, always.

You accumulate experiences and the mind divides them into one of three categories: negative is always registered, positive is understood as an expected event, very positive is always registered. You have to overdo happy in order to have it gain weight because joy is an expectation of this life experience. Because of this "regular," happy goes unnoticed or barely noticed.

Retrain your mind to focus on the positive. Be aware of when the mind is about to step into doo-doo—meaning negative emotion, negative reminders, negative experiences—and steer clear of it.

In the example that we gave with all the jams, the mind could say, "Wow, I love strawberry jam and I think I'd like blueberry jam or boysenberry jam, but I don't like apricot. I don't think I'd like that. I don't like jelly either, but I do like jam."

We like our doo-doo euphemism here because you are adding the do-nots with the dos. Instead, keep with the positive and you will be more likely to reach extra-positive.

"I like blackberry, I like raspberry, I like strawberry, I like grape. I like—I like any kind. I like crab-apple jam. I don't even know if that exists, but I'm sure I would like it."

Do you see how we just made it up? When you practice this technique the mind learns that the better experience is to not combine positive and negative. And then the mind starts to help you with your list of positive things. It is, after all, all about quantity of thought combined with quality of thought. It is just practice. Do the practice, it is well worth it. A mind that is happy is easily trained by the Guide to hear us.

End chapter.

CHAPTER 5

Ocularity is Me, Myself, and My Guide

"*The mind does not know what you are wanting. It simply knows what you have been paying attention to.*"

Session 5
Channeled April 11, 2021

Ocularity

Intuitive, clairvoyant, channeling is the human being's current vernacular for what we are calling ocularity. Those are the resultant factors that occur from someone who has enhanced their capability to have communication with us. Everyone is a "psychic." Okay, no you are not. But yes, you acquire it from being in this world.

We are writing several chapters today, and the last chapter Carol was sitting on her balcony. She got cold and decided to go indoors where she would feel comfortable and could sit and have numerous sessions with us. She chose the living room and then once she sat down, the cat got on her lap and we began. And then we stopped talking.

Interiorly (meaning ocularly), we told her she liked it better on the balcony. She thought we were simply giving her information and taking a momentary break from dictation. We had to stop, however, because her mind was not wanting to be indoors. Her MIND was not wanting to be indoors although it was not the one choosing indoors or outdoors, it simply knew that it was happy and then was not as happy. We saw in her mind that it was moving into a position that would be more difficult to say the words we wanted. We could have chosen to ask for a break, but we also knew that simply moving back outside would remedy the issue. She carefully weighed the pros and cons of going back outside and then preference arose—the preference to believe we know all things. To believe that if her mind was happier outside, then being outside at that moment was better for her.

This is an example of someone who has learned from us and about us. It is someone who has learned to trust who she is communicating with. It is not easy to do this. It is all too easy for doubt to rise up in the active mind. Learning to trust us can teach the mind to respond to our teaching with love, attention, patience, and then you lovely students will hear us.

We discuss ocular verbal receiving now. Many of you trust what you hear, but you should not because the mind has a way of contaminating the message. We say hello and it tells you that we said hello or, we say hello and it says, "Hi. How are you doing? I'm Johnny." We did not say all of that or perhaps not any of it, but the mind produced something as though we had. Alternatively, we may say hello and it produces an image of a rock or it says nothing because the mind is in the early stages of LEARNING how to transfer knowing into seeing or hearing...accuracy must be learned. None of you are accurate in the beginning.

Who among you knows for sure that what you hear in your mind, presumably from us, is accurate? Not one of you. Not one of you. You do not know for sure. You have experiences that indicate you might be accurate or might be inaccurate depending on validation from others. But you do not know for certain if what you see or hear is what was sent to you. We do. We know for sure how accurate you are in any given moment.

Sometimes the mind is weak—you might be physically tired, stressors are about, or people are about, or money is involved, or friends and family are involved because you try to give readings to people. When you sit down to receive all by yourself and you just play a game called Show Me a Picture or any other technique, you teach yourself to not worry about being right.

When you sit down and you ask us to tell you a story or give you evidential information so that you can prove to yourself and others that you are accurate, well, you teach the mind that you need to be right. The mind wants to please you and so it starts to give you a little bit to see how you do with it. If you like it, it gives you a little bit more. If you like it a lot, it starts to give you a lot.

What is it giving you? Anything. At least at first. It, your interior mind, makes it up. It is hard to understand in the beginning that the mind is not accurate. Accuracy is learned over time. It receives some from us and adds to it or it selects something from your own memory banks and presents it to you as being from us. You do not know which it is—accurate or inaccurate. We do.

This field of vision that the inner mind has is more vast than you can fathom. Its vision has no time nor space limitation. It sees thoughts—all of them. A sea of thoughts. If you were to see the date/time stamp of all of the thoughts that your mind has in it in any thirty-second snapshot, most of it would be outside the span of years that you have been alive. For example, the physical space that you are sitting or standing in while you are reading this particular page has been in existence for millenniums with life and life forms that have been on that patch of dirt for all of it.

Your twenty; thirty; fifty; sixty; ninety-five years do not even scratch the surface on the number of memories that are resident in your perceived experience. The interior mind sees thoughts. It sees triangulation. It sees commonality. It sees quantity. It sees thoughts. These thoughts cannot talk to it, they just be. These thoughts are also in the memory bank of you and are subject to retrieval.

Thoughts, they are like soap bubbles. In cartoons, they show little people inside a soap bubble having a conversation. The soap bubble contains a moment in time and an emotional equivalent layer around it and an emotional cord hanging from it. When you are wanting to know something, you do not know how the information finds you. It is the interior mind that finds it for you and then draws it to you. We see what the mind is looking at based on the things that you say or talk about or pay attention to and we see what it is reaching for. We see the soap bubble that it has in its line of sight, and we see the timeline of how long it will take the mind to touch it, meaning manifest it for you. We see how many obstacles are in the way. Those obstacles can be positive or negative.

If it is reaching for some delightful new thing and you have resistance in the way, that is a negative obstacle. If you have had a bad day and are not trying to change it, you are reaching for an even worse evening. But if you have had a really good week, well, that really bad evening has positive roadblocks—or, opportunities—that will help it avoid reaching for that worse evening.

When you are in a momentary bad mood and you have had a bad mood preceding it, you are on your way to a worse evening. There are things to do that can sway your mind from it, but if you do not instill them you probably will not